More HANDBELLS for the CHRISTIAN YEAR

Sondra Tucker

Abingdon Press

CONTENTS

Title	Octaves	Season(s)	Page
People, Look East	2 or 3	*Advent*	3
O Holy Night	2 or 3 (with keyboard)	*Christmas*	
Full Score			6
Handbell Score			13
Sweet Hour of Prayer	2	*Lent (General)*	16
Hallelujah Chorus	2 or 3	*General (Christmas, Easter)*	20
O Sons and Daughters	2 or 3	*Easter*	27
Christ the Lord Is Risen Today	2 or 3 (with organ)	*Easter*	
Fulll Score			30
Handbell Score			36
To God Be the Glory	3	*Pentecost (Ascension, General)*	39
Chaconne	2 or 3	*General*	42
Trumpet Tune	3	*General (Weddings)*	45

Copyright © 1995 Abingdon Press

All rights reserved.

This book is printed on acid-free, recycled paper.

All rights on all materials are reserved by Abingdon Press and no part of this work may be reproduced or transmitted in any form or by any means, electronic or mechanical, including photocopying and recording, or by any storage and retrieval system, except as may be expressly permitted in the 1976 Copyright Act or in writing from the publisher. Requests for permission should be addressed in writing to Permissions Office, The United Methodist Publishing House, 201 Eighth Avenue, South, Nashville, Tennessee 37203.

ISBN 0-687-01003-9

Manufactured in the United States of America

People, Look East

French Carol
arr. by Sondra Tucker

Two-octave choirs omit notes in parentheses ( ).
Three-octave choirs omit notes in brackets [ ].

Arr. © 1995 Abingdon Press

*Staccato eighth notes played with mallets (bells on table, not held)

6

O Holy Night
For Two- or Three-Octave Handbells and Keyboard

Full Score

Adolphe Adam
arr. by Sondra Tucker

Two-octave choirs omit notes in parentheses ( ).

Arr. © 1995 Abingdon Press

O Holy Night

2 or 3 octaves
Handbells used: (18) (26)

Handbell Score

Adophe Adam
arr. by Sondra Tucker

Andante (♩. = 68)

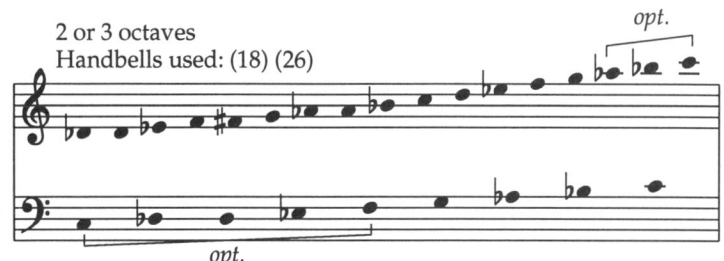

Two-octave choirs omit notes in parentheses ( ).

Arr. © 1995 Abingdon Press

Sweet Hour of Prayer

2 octaves
Handbells used: (24)

William Bradbury
arr. by Sondra Tucker

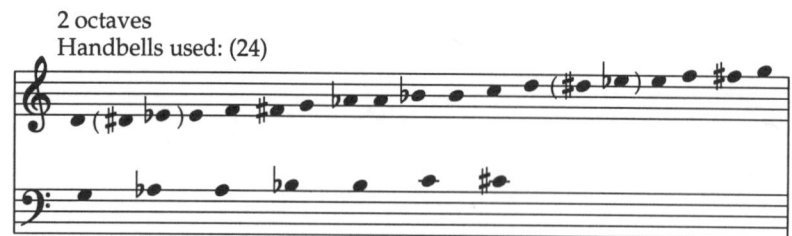

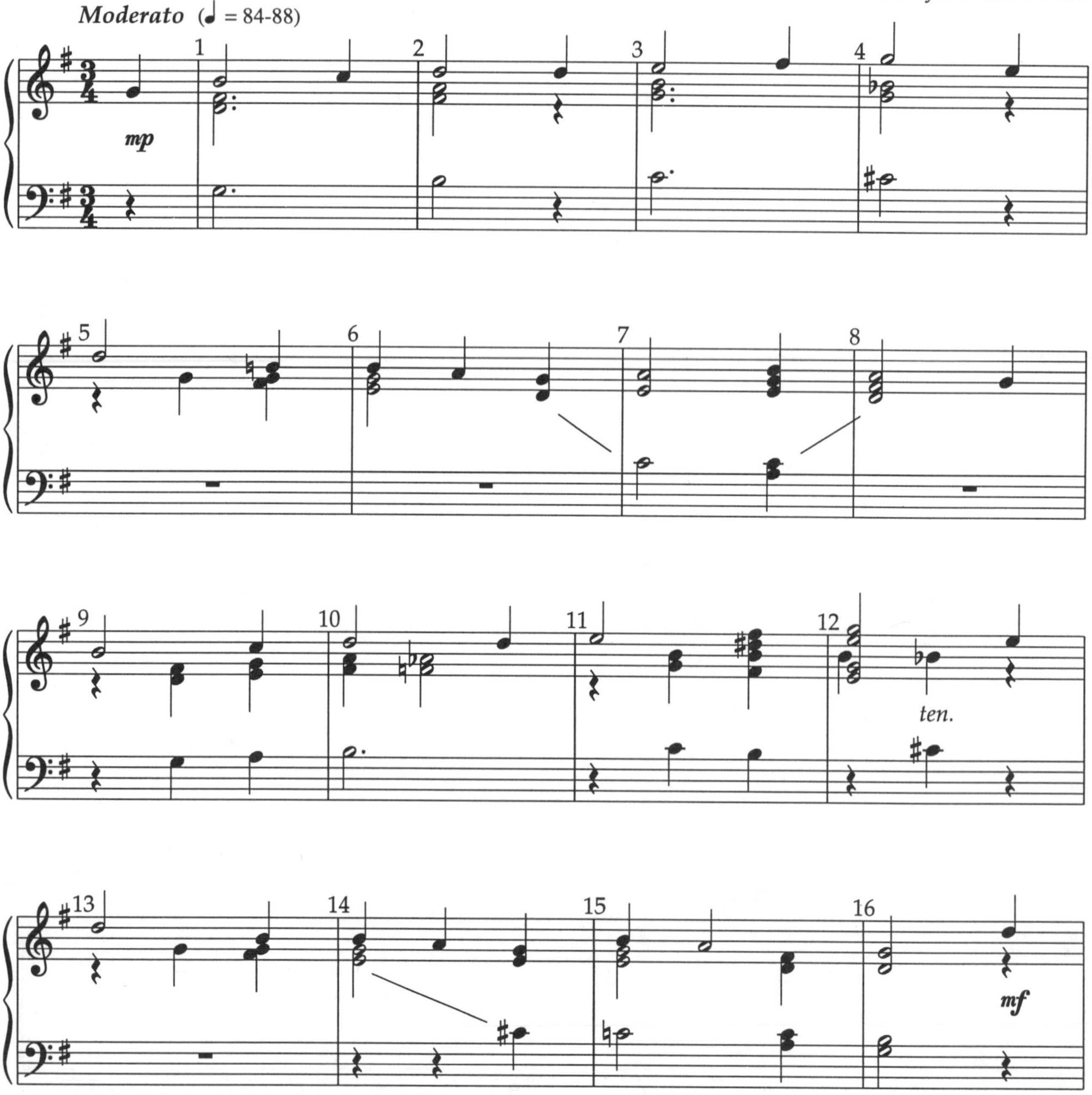

Hallelujah Chorus

George F. Handel
arr. by Sondra Tucker

Two-octave choirs omit notes in parentheses ( ).
Three-octave choirs omit notes in brackets [ ].

Arr. © 1995 Abingdon Press

O Sons and Daughters

15th cent. French carol
arr. by Sondra Tucker

Two-octave choirs omit notes in parentheses ( ).

Arr. © 1995 Abingdon Press

* LV for notes with stems up (tenor).

Christ the Lord Is Risen Today
Hymn Accompaniment for Organ and Two- or Three-Octave Handbells

Full Score

Lyra Davidica
arr. by Sondra Tucker

Two-octave choirs omit notes in parentheses ( ).

Arr. © 1995 Abingdon Press

Christ the Lord Is Risen Today

Handbell Score

Lyra Davidica
arr. by Sondra Tucker

Two-octave choir omit notes in parentheses ( ).

Arr. © 1995 Abingdon Press

Play first time only.

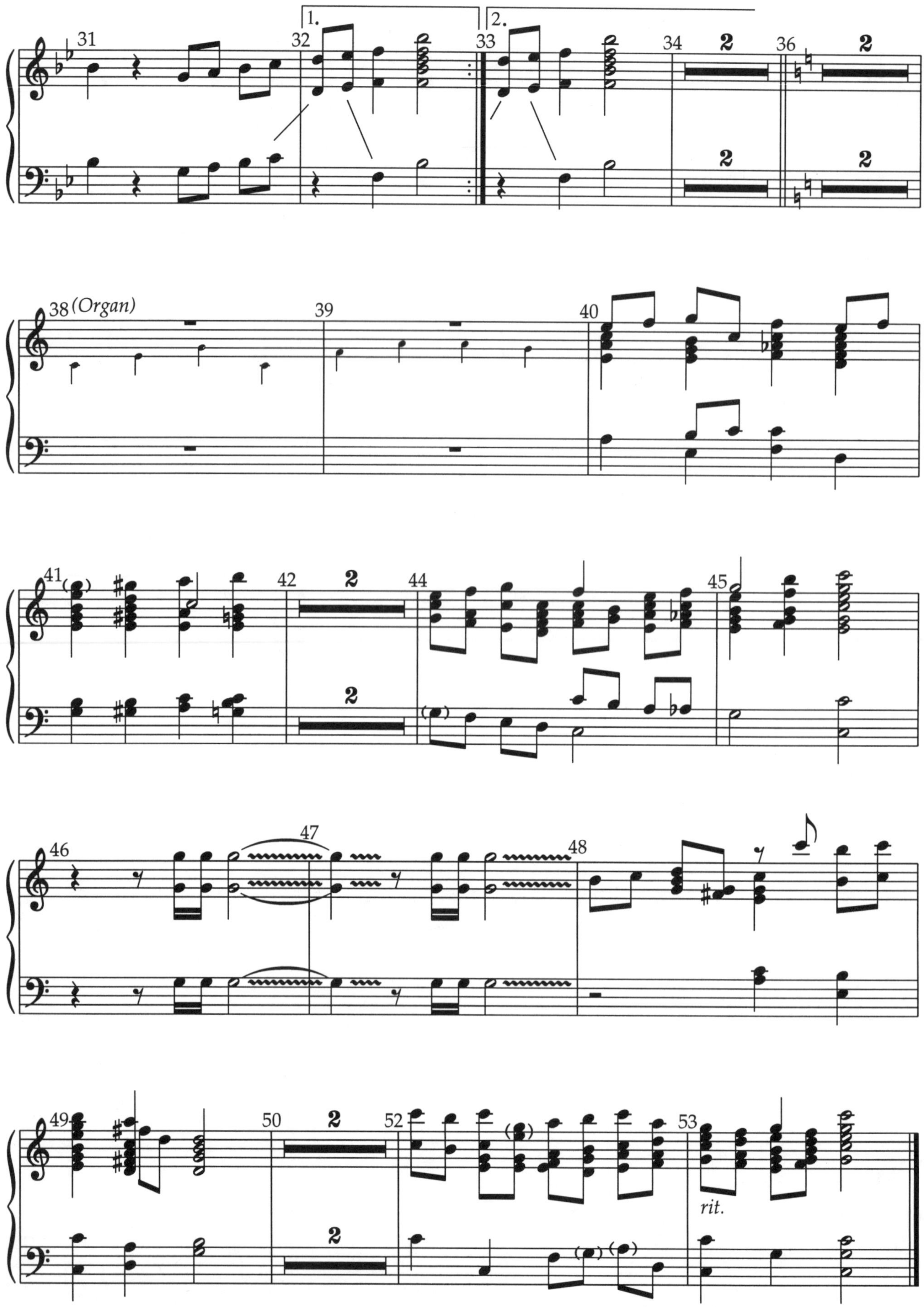
1.
2.
(Organ)
rit.

To God Be the Glory

3 octaves
Handbells used: (31)

Allegro (♩ = 116)

William H. Doane
arr. by Sondra Tucker

Arr © 1995 Abingdon Press

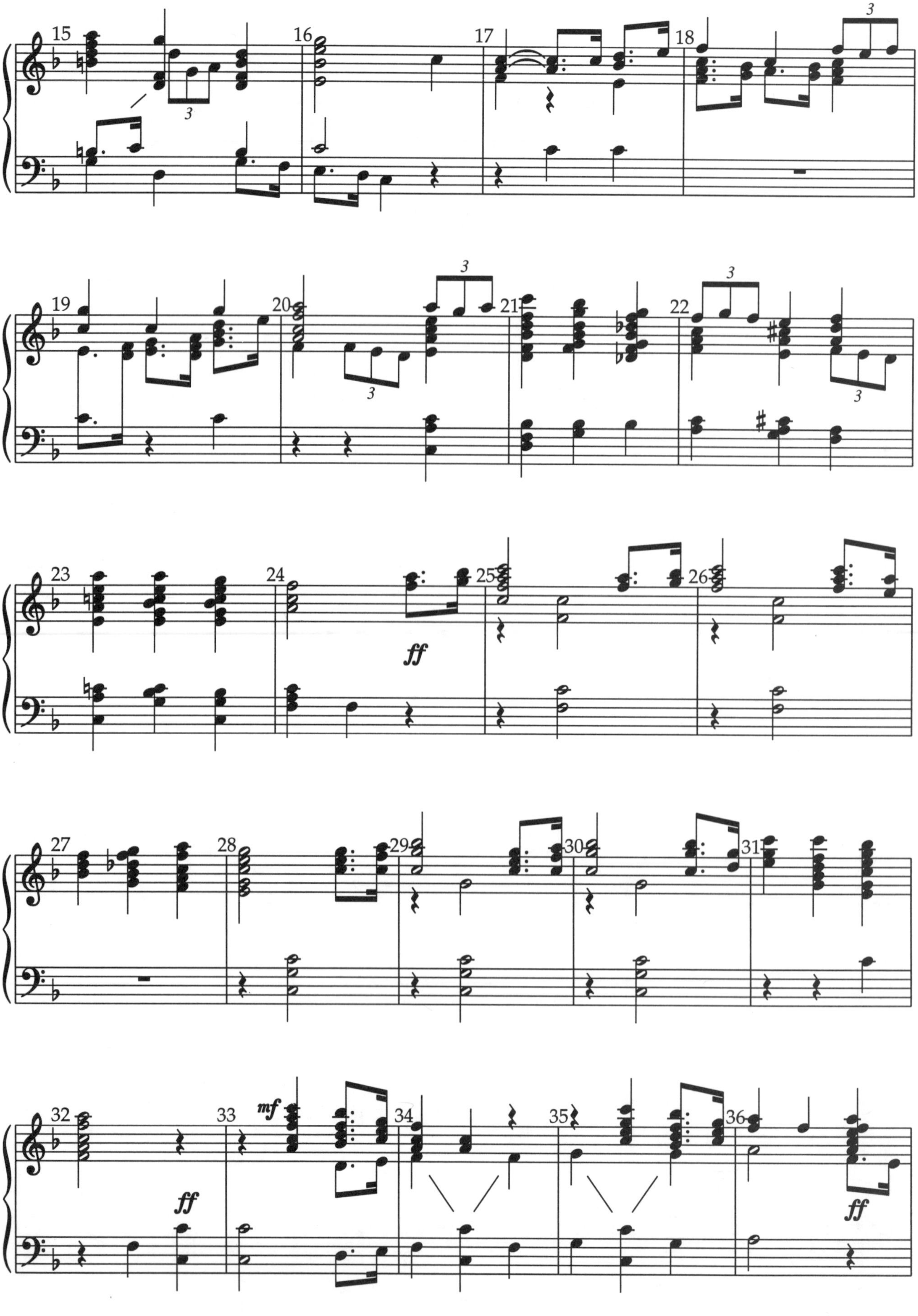
ff
ff
mf
ff

41

Chaconne

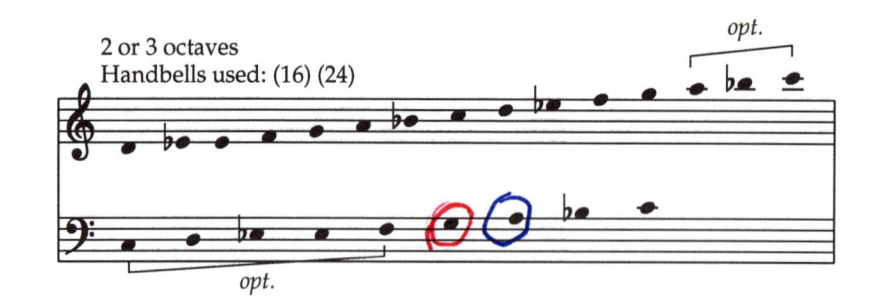

2 or 3 octaves
Handbells used: (16) (24)

Henry Purcell
arr. by Sondra Tucker

Andante ($\quarternote = 72$)

pp - p

mp - mf

Two-octave choirs omit notes in parentheses ( ).

Arr. © 1995 Abingdon Press

43

44

Trumpet Tune

3 octaves
Handbells used: (25)

Henry Purcell
arr. by Sondra Tucker

Maestoso (♩ = 72)

Arr. © 1995 Abingdon Press

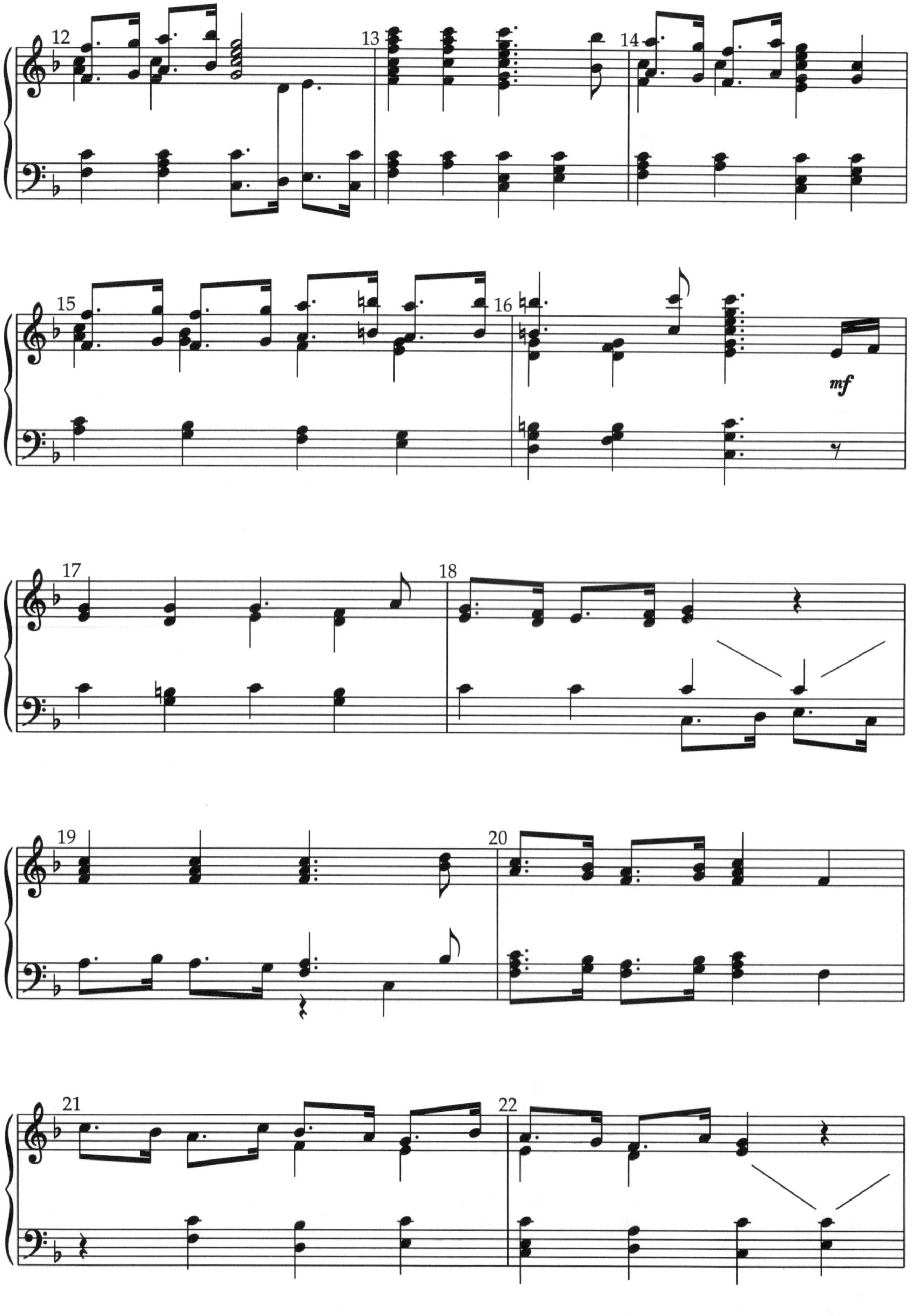
12
13
14
15
16
mf
17
18
19
20
21
22

47